IMPRESSIONIST
PAINTING

S0-ALD-497

IMPRESSIONIST PAINTING

by *Albert Châtelet*

Director, Lille Museum, France

McGRAW-HILL BOOK COMPANY

New York   Toronto   London   Sydney

Copyright © 1962 by the McGraw-Hill Book Company, Inc.
All rights reserved. Printed in the United States of America.
This book, or parts thereof, may not be reproduced in any
form without permission of the publishers.
Library of Congress Catalog Card Number: 62-18981
10710

VIII

IMPRESSIONIST PAINTING

The art of impressionism conjures up a world of magical charm filled with light and color. In its scintillating canvases we encounter vivid strokes of color, brilliant skies, golden coppery waters, and happy boaters flirting with some pretty girl in the semishade of a teagarden. It is an art that adds brilliance to such museums as the Jeu de Paume in Paris, the Art Institute of Chicago, and the celebrated collections of the Metropolitan Museum of Art in New York, the Museum of Fine Arts in Boston, the Phillips Collection in Washington, and the Barnes Collection in Merion, Pennsylvania.

Although the fascinating term, impressionism, challenges our power to define it, we can identify the artists who may be considered impressionists. Among them are Manet, Degas, Monet, Renoir, Bazille, Sisley, Morisot, and Cassatt. These remain distinct from such other artists as Cézanne, Gauguin, Van Gogh, Seurat, Signac, or Toulouse-Lautrec, who may rather be called postimpressionists.

The impressionist painters expressed no clear artistic theory and signed no manifesto. Thus, in order to determine the significance of this movement, we must begin by exploring the story of the artists' interrelationships and their artistic evolution.

The story has often been told of how the word "impressionist" actually came about. In 1874 a group of painters who called themselves simply an "association of painters, sculptors, and engravers" opened a show in the old studio of the photographer Nadar. Among the works displayed was one by Monet, which he entitled in the catalogue, *Impression, Rising Sun.* The art critic of *Charivari,* Louis Leroy, used Monet's painting as an excuse to deride these artists in a satirical article which he entitled "Exhibition of the Impressionists." Ironically, the word applied by Leroy captivated those against whom it was directed. They began to use the word too, and later art criticism recognized it as an expressive term for their art.

Only the name, however, was born in 1874, and we must go further back in time to discover the origin of the movement. The artists who exhibited together in 1874 had already joined forces during the preceding decade. Eleven years earlier, in 1863, the jury of the official salon — where every French artist hoped to gain recognition by showing his works — had proved to be particularly harsh in its artistic judgment. Under pressure of a general uproar from those artists whose works had been rejected, the Emperor Napoleon III ordered an exhibition for those refused, the so-called *Salon des Refusés,* which included all the works excluded from the official salon.

The exhibition proved a scandal to bourgeois society, and two works especially seemed to symbolize in its eyes the "bad taste" of their authors: *The Woman in White* by Whistler and *Luncheon on the Grass* by Manet (*see color slide*). The American Whistler went his own way and remained apart from the artists who concern us here. Manet, however, attracted the attention of a group of young men who saw him, more or less consciously, as their master. The group at first consisted of several students at the École des Beaux-Arts who worked — somewhat against their inclinations — in the studio of the official painter Gleyre: Claude Monet, Auguste Renoir, Frédéric Bazille, and Alfred

Sisley. Soon an older artist, Edgar Degas, only two years Manet's junior, would join them, even though he had been a student of Lamotte and an ardent disciple of Ingres. The group would eventually include a few artists who had gathered together in the free studio of Monsieur Suisse, where one studied a model without having to submit to the corrections of an academic professor: Camille Pissarro, Armand Guillaumin, and Paul Cézanne.

What did these painters of such diverse backgrounds see in Manet? Nothing more, doubtless, than the leader of a new realist school. Not, certainly, a realism of the kind exploited by Courbet, whose paintings were considered shocking because of the presumable vulgarity of their subject matter, and who placed his realism in scenes of the countryside. Manet, on the contrary, accepted the contemporary world, not hesitating to paint the society about him while rejecting the allegorical, mythological, or historical themes that still dominated official art.

Indeed, Manet represented the artist described by Baudelaire as truly "modern," who "knows exactly how to see and understand us as grand and poetic beings dressed in ties and polished boots." As a matter of fact, in 1863, at the Martinet Gallery, Manet exhibited a work that seemed perfectly in accord with this doctrine of contemporaneity: *Music in the Tuileries* (*Figure 1*), where, according to Antonin Proust, one could often observe him at work with Baudelaire looking on.

But it was not only the contemporary scene, or "modernity," that fascinated Manet; he also developed a new technique in painting. Manet filled his shadows with colors, contrary to the academicians who indicated shadows by careful gradations of the local tone. Manet's palette was, above all, a light one, certainly much lighter than the somber harmonies then in vogue, and he strove to evoke a sense of the outdoors. Three years later, Zola understood this precisely when he wrote: "I have again seen *Luncheon on the Grass* and I challenge any of our painters now in fashion to paint a horizon with as much breadth or with as

On the following page
Figure 1. Manet:
Music at the Tuileries.
London, National Gallery

much air and light as can be seen in this painting. Yes, you laugh at this because you have been so taken by the violet skies of M. Nazon. But there is in this work of Manet a nature so beautifully constructed that it will most assuredly displease you. Furthermore, we have here neither the Cleopatra in plaster of M. Gérôme nor the pretty rose and white figures of M. Dubufe; we find instead everyday people who suffer the mistake of having been born with muscles and bones like everyone else."

"Realism" (although to avoid confusion with Courbet's art, "modernism" would be a better word), "light painting," "outdoor painting" seem to be the terms that best unite the painters who saw Manet as their leader. Some of them, however, such as Degas, hesitated to go the way of Manet. Degas, for example, still dreamed of the day when he would make a name for himself as a painter of history. He composed, with a view to the official salons, such works as *Semiramis Constructing a Village* or *The Misfortunes of the Village of Orléans (Figure 2)*. But this ambition did not stop him from becoming attracted to the world around him. Beginning in 1867, he composed some portraits in

Figure 2. Degas: The Misfortunes of the Village of Orléans. Paris, Louvre Museum, galleries of the Jeu de Paume

8

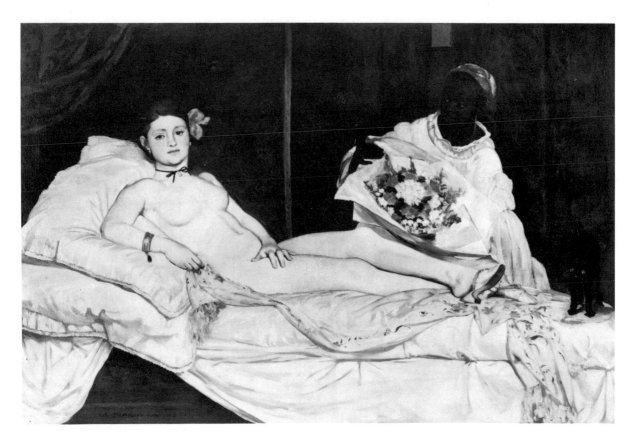

*Figure 3. Manet:
Olympia. Paris,
Louvre Museum,
galleries of the
Jeu de Paume*

a real "modernism" which interpreted the model not merely through her physical appearance but more through the surroundings in which she lived and through the small accessories of her daily life.

Manet, in the years before the war of 1870, concentrated only on the "modern" aspect of his style. He went so far as to interpret the subjects of the old masters in a contemporary environment. Thus, in 1865 he exhibited at the salon what was to become a scandalous painting, his *Olympia* (*Figure 3*), which appeared as an interpretation in modern terms of Titian's *Venus of Urbino*. In the same way, his painting *The Balcony* recalls Goya's *Maja on the Balcony*.

Nevertheless, apart from all innovation, Manet is a painter in the fullest sense of that word. He expresses his ideas through his brushes, by the values of his color harmonies, and through the delicacy of his greys. His themes are really excuses for composing in paint, rather than ends in themselves. His works are of the first rank therefore, not so much because of the persons they might depict or the stories they might tell, but because of their intrinsic qualities.

There soon appeared on the scene a young woman, Berthe Morisot, who wanted to become his student. Before coming to his studio, she had been asking for instruction from Corot. Also, she was more attracted to landscape and outdoor painting than was Manet, and was more receptive to the similar artistic endeavors that went on around her. Morisot's art is a completely feminine variation of Manet's, more delicate in its harmonies, more refined in its drawing. But it creates at the same time a link between her vision and that of certain young artists, friends of hers, who were investigating the effects of light in the atmosphere.

It was not, then, with Manet or with Degas that the real ferment of the new artistic movement was generated. We must turn rather to Monet and Renoir, on one hand, and to Pissarro on the other. Pissarro was essentially a landscape painter who pursued further the ideas of Corot and Daubigny, thereby eventually evolving to a point where he rejected the tradition of landscapes composed within the confines of a studio, in the hope of convincing the public to accept as complete those works executed out of doors. The painter soon became interested in a lightening of his palette; his work outdoors led him to prefer full light and clear color relationships to the traditional half tones.

Monet, for his part, seemed to become obsessed by the *Luncheon on the Grass* or, more exactly, by his apparent ambition to interpret figures in their environment and in the light of

Figure 4. Monet:
Luncheon on the Grass.
Courtesy,
Durand-Ruel, Paris

outdoors. At the same time, he realized suddenly how, from this point of view, the work of the elder master, Manet, was imperfect. He wanted to bring to fruition this particular concept. In 1865 he worked in the forest of Fontainebleau on a great and new *Luncheon on the Grass (Figure 4)*, a work which was never finished but the concept of which is preserved for us in a small canvas (only two fragments remain of the original). In 1866, he undertook and this time completed his *Women in the Garden (see color slide)*, which followed the same idea. In these two works, he assumes without hesitation the consequences of his theme: his figures are swallowed by great puddles of bluish

Figure 5. Bazille: Woman in a Pink Dress. Montpellier, Fabre Museum

Figure 6. Bazille:
Family Portrait.
Courtesy Wadsworth
Atheneum, Hartford

shadows or by brilliant light that erases the masses, reducing
them to silhouettes.

Monet is also followed in this path by his friend Bazille who
attempts the same thing in his *Pink Dress* (*Figure 5*), his *View
of the Village,* or in his *Family Portrait* (*Figure 6*). But Bazille,
less bold than Monet, does not dare destroy a sense of volume
in so radical a fashion. He expresses himself, consequently, in a
kind of dry technique wherein traditional drawing is curiously
juxtaposed to a palette that incorporates sharp contrasts of
shadows and full light.

Renoir, too, faces the same problem, notably in 1867 with
his portrait of *Lisa in a White Robe*; in 1868 with *Sisley and His
Wife*; and still again in 1873 in his great Amazon in the *Bois de*

Figure 7. Renoir: Bather with Dog. São Paulo Museum

14

Boulogne. Meanwhile, he is still often tempted by "official art," as witness, for example, his *Bather with Dog (Figure 7)*.

Impressionist art was destined to develop along this path. Monet, with his figures in the outdoors, developed the landscape that Boudin, in Le Havre, had at first explored. The study of figures led Monet to pay more attention to the play of light, and he turned naturally to studying them within the environment in which he placed them.

Landscapes thus begin to have more and more importance in his work as well as in the work of Renoir and Sisley. These painters with their interest in landscape fit into a great tradition which, since the end of the eighteenth century, had given France a number of landscapists, from Moreau and Valenciennes to Corot and Daubigny, not to mention other painters of the Barbizon School.

Interestingly, in 1802, when Valenciennes wrote his treatise on landscape, he had suggested not only that the painter study the subject carefully out of doors, but that notations be made of the subject at different hours of the day; he underlined, therefore, the importance of light.

Little by little the significance of these studies became apparent to each artist. Corot, the first of them, doubtless raised to the rank of art, in the public mind, his best known canvases painted out of doors in direct contact with nature. The impressionists completed this evolution, and even their studies of changing light — which Valenciennes had treated as mere exercises — would become works of art in themselves.

In 1869, Monet and Renoir worked in Bougival. They set up their easels near La Grenouillère (*Figure 8*), a kind of teagarden that served for both rendezvous and sport among boaters and bathers along the Seine. But the painters were now faced with a new problem: that of translating into paint the reflections on the water and the sparkling of the sun on the moving surface. For unquestionably the first time the painters used juxtaposed touches of paint, unconnected by half tones or moderated passages of color. Through the contrast of these tones, they created a many-hued vibration which becomes a pictorial equivalent of the scintillating quality of the river. One must see these works as the decisive stage of impressionism: they lead the artists, already taken with the idea of painting outdoors, toward the expression of these vibrant luminous phenomena.

The war that broke out in 1870 temporarily dispersed the group. Manet and Degas remained in Paris, but Bazille went to the front and fell in combat on November 28 at Beaume la Rolands. He died without having been able to participate in the full development of the movement. Renoir, also drafted into the army, afterwards suffered severe illness. Monet went to England, where he joined Pissarro.

This stay in England, followed with a trip to Holland by Monet, permitted the two artists to pursue their work in landscape painting. The dense London fog attracted Monet for the first time, and he immediately set to work to interpret in paint the impression of the sun piercing the haze. It has often been said that this sojourn also gave Monet the chance to see the works of Turner and to become immersed in them. Yet it is difficult to discern the influence of the great English master on Monet's works of the succeeding months and years. In all likelihood, the romantic spirit which so profoundly marks the work of Turner troubled Monet, preventing him from assimilating fully those elements in Turner which closely approached his own experimental ideas.

After the war the painters got together again, took up their work in common — and also their discussions. Monet went to Argenteuil in 1871, where he attracted a good many of his friends who, in their turn, would often take as a subject for their paintings the shores of the Seine and its sailing boats. The fol-

Figure 8.   Monet:
La Grenouillère.
New York, Metropolitan
Museum of Art,
The H. O. Havemeyer
Collection

lowing year Pissarro set himself up at Pontoise, where he was soon to be joined by Cézanne.

This period, lasting until 1880-1884, is the time of greatest homogeneity in the movement. The art historian and critic, Lionello Venturi, does not hesitate to define this period as the only real impressionist one. It is a time, also, when a number of ties unite the members of the group. In 1874 they exhibited together for the first time, although without Manet, who still hoped to be recognized and enthroned by the official salon. In 1876, 1877, 1879, and 1880, the artists continued their exhibitions, but three more showings given after the last date lacked the same spirit of unity. A merchant, Paul Durand-Ruel, whom Monet and Pissarro had met in London, became interested in their art and acted not only as the painters' sole dealer but also as their friend and principal supporter. Also, in 1874, Manet and Berthe Morisot came into a closer relationship when Morisot married Manet's brother. She was later to become an important link in the group because of her friendship with Degas and her sympathetic attitude toward the art of Monet and Renoir.

At the time of the third exhibition of the impressionists in 1877, Paul Duranty, a writer and art critic, dedicated a pamphlet to them, entitled, "The New Painting." This study projected a view which seems to have been inspired by Degas and which was badly received by his friends. Yet it was the only comment written in that period of great impressionist activity and unity that clearly explained their aspirations.

We may note particularly in this valuable work a most significant passage describing the goal which the impressionists would thenceforth pursue: "The impressionists have made a discovery in color which has no origin in the works of the Dutch, nor in the clear tones of fresco, nor in the light tonalities of the eighteenth century. They are not solely preoccupied with the simple and supple play of colorations that results from observing the most delicate values in tones which either oppose or penetrate one another. The discovery consists in recognizing that strong light takes away the color of tones, that the sun reflected by objects of nature, because of its intensity, forms these tones into a luminous unity which dissolves the prismatic rays into a single colorless brilliance that we call light. From intuition to intuition, they have been able little by little to decompose sunlight into its rays, into its elements, and to recompose its unity by the general harmony of rainbow colors which they pour out on their canvases. From the point of view of visual delicacy and subtle penetration of colors, it is an altogether extraordinary feat. The most knowledgeable physicist would be unable to criticize their analysis of light."

This important text is particularly revealing in the way it describes in progressive steps the "discovery" of the impressionists. First of all, it places the experiments of the impressionists in the realm of color and emphasizes the exceptional lightness of their new palette. It underlines the fact that the artists in 1877 are still guided by the preoccupation which in 1863 caused them to assert their desire for "clear painting." It is this interest, then, which turned them toward the study of light and of its color effects. And it is this last study that leads them to paint separate touches of pure color, which by their contrasts and their complementary relationships, cause the eye to recreate light or, rather, the total luminous impression in its unity.

Outdoor impressionism may be described, therefore, as the art of enveloping a subject in an atmosphere of pure shimmering color. In order to achieve this effect, the impressionist artists developed a technique of bringing together little spots of unmixed colors that would reinforce each other. Thus they were able to produce a highly light-charged, flickering, and momentary "impression" of the object viewed.

In Duranty's text we may also note the first suggestion of a scientific analysis of light. But we must not, as has sometimes been done, take this particular reference too literally. It was, in fact, Seurat and his later "pointillist" friends who really worked with a palette in which everything was reduced to the fundamental colors of the sunlight prism and who exploited pictorially the observations of the physicists. The impressionists certainly knew something about the laws of light — at least through the art historian Charles Blanc — but they never disciplined themselves rigorously along scientific lines. They chose rather to allow their artistic instincts to guide them, or their "intuition" (which is the term Duranty used to describe their process).

As we have seen, then, the overriding preoccupation of the impressionists in 1877 consisted of the same elements that had captured their interest in 1863: clear painting and painting outdoors. The concept of "modernism" became less important, except in the cases of Degas and Manet who remained firmly attached to this idea.

The moment the painters emphasized the expression of light, the less important did the subject become. Monet, in 1872, by calling one of his paintings, *Impression, Rising Sun*, refuses in effect to call it *Le Havre*, which is the actual port to which the painting refers. Monet's aim is to present to us the colored impression created before his eyes by the sun rising in the mist. It is a subjective art in the sense that it represents a totally personal vision of the painter. It is an art, too, which can be called fugitive in the sense that it captures a luminous effect at a specific fleeting moment in time.

Monet develops his ideas by using many varied themes, but during his time at Argenteuil he prefers to find those subjects which can best display the phenomena of light vibration: at first water, then snow, then fog, mist, and smoke. The shores of the Seine at Argenteuil are among his favorites with their great white boat sails. He chooses, also, the snow at Vétheuil or the puffs of locomotive smoke in the Saint-Lazare railroad station.

Monet's position may be distinguished from that of his friends; he actually became more systematic in his approach,

*Figure 9. Sisley:
Flood at Marly Port.
Paris, Louvre Museum,
galleries of the
Jeu de Paume*

even more theoretical — though he never wrote about it. It was not by chance that he named one of his paintings as he did, a painting which served as a kind of baptism for himself and his friends. Beginning with some of his canvases executed in London in 1870-1871, luminous effects became his essential focal point of interest. From then on he abandoned almost entirely any interest in the figure, which up until that time had been his chosen theme. Landscapes became his passion, landscapes bathed in light in which forms seemed to dissolve into one another through the effect of the vibrations created by the touches of color.

Monet's friends did not approach his ideas quite so closely. Sisley, although he often seems quite close to Monet, remains faithful to a specific definition of forms even in such works as those dealing with the *Flood at Marley Port (Figure 9)* — perhaps his greatest masterpiece. His works are characterized by a refinement of technique that makes him the "little master" of impressionism. He expresses his ideas with the most delicate nuances.

Pissarro also remained faithful to his interest in landscape which, indeed, he had embraced before Monet. But Pissarro did not remain close to Monet, in fact, less so than Sisley. Pissarro's works show a solid construction which defines clearly all areas in his paintings. Before 1873, he had become interested in the constructive forms of the generation of Corot and Daubigny: the receding lines of a road, a river, or a valley.

After 1873, this desire to arrive at some kind of specific construction within his painting became even more accentuated by the influence of his friend Paul Cézanne. For if it is true that Pissarro had opened Cézanne's eyes to impressionism, the latter most assuredly brought much to Pissarro. In 1873 Cézanne went to Auvers-sur-Oise, not far from where Pissarro was residing in Pontoise. The two friends saw much of each other and often worked together, frequently finding themselves taken under the wing of that strange amateur in art, Dr. Gachet. Until now, Cézanne, the painter from Aix, had worked in a romantic style, even what we might call today baroque, evoking mysterious and often sensual scenes modeled in large blocks of paint that create a muted effect. At Auvers his palette changed: he adopted the clear tones of the impressionists, and landscapes became his favorite subject. He strove to be an impressionist; he was, in fact, "impressionist" for some months, but even so, his works were strongly composed, and each element was placed clearly and emphatically in perspective.

Figure 10. Pissarro:
Maison Delafolie.
Boston,
Museum of Fine Arts

Pissarro was also obsessed with this idea of form but not quite so systematically as was his friend. Pissarro combined his interest in solid forms in perspective with the ideas of the impressionists, creating an art wherein all elements are kept in a careful balance (*Figure 10*). Through his wish to define forms clearly in a completely discernible design, he kept alive the ideas of Corot and Daubigny. He is truly an impressionist, however, in his use of a delicate touch and the contrast of pure tones. But in his care for composition he escapes somewhat the impressionists' overriding interest in ephemeral phenomena, thereby making contact with the postimpressionist painters.

Renoir was really the painter closest to Monet during this period at Argenteuil, staying with him for long periods of time. Certain works of the two painters were executed together on the same site, using an almost identical light and composition (*Figures 11, 12*). Renoir, however, never abandoned his first love, the human figure, which he painted more than landscape. It is first of all the figure of a woman that Renoir paints in all the glory of her body or in all the grace of her feminine poses. More than Monet's own *Women in the Garden*, Renoir's *Nude in the Sun* (*see color slide*) is the fulfillment of the idea behind Manet's *Luncheon on the Grass*: an evocation of the human figure out of doors. Renoir truly revitalizes the academic tradition. It is living flesh that he paints; the skin colors burning in a blaze of sunshine or muted by the interwoven patterns of heavy foliage.

Renoir paints joyous, happy people: gay dancers of the *Moulin de la Galette* (*see color slide*), an elegant woman in *The Swing*, or friendly boaters in the painting at the Phillips Collection. Renoir, more than any of his other colleagues, realized that impressionism was an art of joy and well-being. Serenity, a relaxed air, joy itself and often eager, discreet sensuality — such are the sentiments that impregnate his works and that dominate also the landscapes of his friends. There is no trace of their struggle or painful searching in the art of these impressionists; rather, a serenity and voluptuousness, if not luxury, seems the essence of their work.

During this happy period at Argenteuil, only Degas and Manet continued to work more closely to tradition. Manet, though, perhaps through the intervention of Berthe Morisot, allowed himself to be caught up in the interests of his young friends at Argenteuil. Following their example, he lightened and made more brilliant his palette which up until that time was still heavily weighted in favor of cold tones. He even went

Figure 11.   Renoir:
Seine at Argenteuil.
Portland Art Museum,
Ayer Bequest

Figure 12.   Monet:
The Boaters at Argenteuil.
Courtesy, Durand-Ruel
Paris

so far as to loosen his ordinarily disciplined brush work and to essay at times the light and spontaneous techniques of his friends. He had never searched so systematically to interpret the impression of light out of doors as he did in his *In a Boat* or in his portrait of *Monet Painting in His Boat* (*Figure 13*). Moreover, with his persistence in pursuing "modernism," he painted *The Bar at the Folies Bergère* (*Figure 14*). His brush work in this painting carries with it the reflections of the Seine; the forms dilute themselves in the bar mirror, rendering even more sensitively the colored magic of the rays thrown off from the artificial lamps.

It was Degas, finally, who assimilated least the ideas of the group, even though he remained a staunch supporter and a faithful exhibitor at their shows. He did not go to Argenteuil, and rare indeed are any landscapes he painted other than those of race tracks, where he loved to paint galloping horses and elegant riders. For Degas, the contemporary life around him was the

Figure 13. Manet: Monet Painting in His Boat. Munich, Bavarian State Picture Collection

26

Figure 14. Manet: The Bar at the Folies Bergère. London, Courtauld Institute of Art

most important element for his painting. Unconsciously, perhaps, he was nevertheless caught up in some ideas which paralleled those of his friends. He never treats light indifferently in his canvases; on the contrary, he captures light always in a unique and fleeting moment.

Degas is also impressionist in the way he conceives of an impression as the seizing of an ephemeral event: in his works, it is the grace of a race horse, in the display of its walk or its gallop; it is the fleeting beauty of a dancer tracing an arabesque in the air; or it is the play of hands with the elegant and curious shapes of hats in a milliner's workshop (*Figure 15*). Only in Degas's work, however, these evocations express a joy that is somewhat reserved. Beneath the charm of his gestures, under the surface of the purity of his balanced compositions, there is a heavy secret bitterness, an uneasiness that is part of the consciousness of the ephemeral, the transient in life. In Degas, these special moments are not sensed and savored even in their beauty, but are immediately perceived as fleeting. The realization of their irrevocable disappearance is a contemporary sentiment which is also part of their special charm (*Figure 16*).

Close to Degas was Mary Cassatt, an American painter, who then appeared in the impressionist orbit and became associated with them. Her sureness of manner captivated Degas who encouraged and inspired her. Nevertheless, her art is more relaxed, and with its full forms and strong volumes, it comes a bit nearer to Manet.

The fragile unity of this group and the coherence of its approach, attained with such difficulty, could only be precarious. Around 1880, the movement already began to lose its unity. In 1883 Manet died. The same year, Seurat painted his first great work, *The Bather*, in which he turned his back on impressionism, rejecting the spontaneity of vision and substituting a calculated elaboration of an artistic idea. This doctrine would sometimes tempt the patriarch of the impressionists, Pissarro, who was perhaps already sensitive to such an approach through his previous contact with Cézanne. But this influence did not last long; until his death in 1903, Pissarro remained the most faithful and the most moderate of the impressionists. In his last years, Pissarro turned again to the first preoccupations of the impressionists, namely, their interest in modernity, in the contemporary subject. The artist introduced it in his landscapes: his views of Parisian boulevards and his scenes of village life are, in effect, an interpretation of contemporary life in all its vitality and in the excitement of its crowds of people.

Figure 15. Degas:
The Millinery Shop.
The Art Institute of Chicago
Mr. and Mrs. Lewis L. Coburn
Memorial Collection

29

*Figure 16. Degas:
The Bassoonist Dihau
in the Orchestra.
Paris, Louvre Museum,
galleries of the
Jeu de Paume*

But the interest in a more disciplined painting was felt not only by Seurat and his friends. Renoir, for example, went through an "Ingres" crisis between 1883 and 1888 (*see color slide*). He wanted to find a pure treatment, a clarity on canvas, to bring forms to life by delimiting them with a dry line. Although this remained only a short phase in Renoir's work, it profoundly affected his future activity, for henceforth he was never to capture again the spontaneity and direct vision of impressionism. His works were to become more carefully delineated, more completely defined in their formal elements, while also becoming veritable poems in color. This feeling for the good life and physical well-being, which Renoir expressed in such refined harmonies at Argenteuil, explodes now into a festival of hot colors, in a palette where the reds reign supreme, in a kind of painting that emphasizes the power and expressiveness of the color.

This discovery of expressive color, this escape into a more abstract color, was not the accomplishment of Renoir alone. The discovery doubtless germinated in the impressionism of Argenteuil, in that the division of tones on a canvas brought an appreciation of color in its purity and brilliance, a brilliance no longer descriptive or lyrical at this point. It is a strange paradox that Degas became interested in this phase during his last working years. His sight was failing at this time — he shortly became almost blind — and, unconsciously no doubt, he renounced his earlier working habits with their precise techniques worthy of a seventeenth-century Dutch painter, and instead expressed himself in a less disciplined but more suggestive approach to drawing. This transformation was accompanied by the use of more brilliant tones and harmonies so rich in color that they surpassed the impressionist concepts. More than an interpretation of a momentary impression, Degas's later compositions emphasize the expressive idea, giving his work more vigor in its testimony

Figure 17.   Monet:
The Houses of Parliament.
Courtesy, Durand-Ruel,
Paris

of life; later such a concept was to be called postimpressionism.

Monet himself was not far from traveling the path of Renoir and Degas. It is true that he remained faithful to the visual impression, and the better to interpret it in its purity and uniqueness, he undertook a series of paintings which rendered the same subject but under different, changing lights of the same day. He began first with the theme of haystacks, then poplar trees, and finally the portals of Rouen Cathedral. Afterwards, if Monet varied his subjects for a while — from the Houses of Parliament (*Figure 17*) in London to scenes of Venice — it was again in order to paint each of them in a unique light which recreated the subject in form and color. Further, from the beginning of the new century, Monet scarcely left his magnificent garden at Giverny whose lovely lily ponds gave him an ever recurring theme to paint. When he painted his cathedrals, however, it took him almost two years to end up with twenty canvases, and it was in his Paris studio that he achieved the high point of those works, presumably conceived as the direct translation of a fleeting moment. This proves really that the extreme purity sought after by Monet killed his spontaneity and opened the doors to a kind of creation wherein the spirit recovers its dominance over the eye. Here, indeed, is the key to his last evolution in painting, the birth of those astonishing compositions that some have called abstract, where the lily ponds of Giverny are no more than the point of departure, the taking-off place for an imagination which creates on the canvas a colored magic of long, interlaced strokes.

Sisley, usually so self-possessed, allowed himself to follow in the wake of his friend, although he lacked the same creative facility. Berthe Morisot also fell under the spell, creating works of art that express especially the charm of a sinuous stroke, of long ribbons of paint that stretch across the canvas in sweeps and coils akin to the forms of Art Nouveau, especially in the latter's furniture and decoration. Only Mary Cassatt, faithful to

the spirit of Degas, remained attached to an earlier impressionism, near that of Manet, putting it to use in her painting of children.

In the end, the group dispersed — a group whose coherence
could only be called, in any case, a temporary one. Other artists
came into prominence, appearing as new beacons for the young:
Cézanne, already now far from impressionism, Seurat, Gauguin,
Van Gogh, and Toulouse-Lautrec.

But the role of impressionism was decisive. It constituted,
first of all, an artistic break because it rejected the traditional
attributes of art. The impressionist technique did not impose a
rule so much as a new conception of art: a work no longer had
to be "finished" to be of value. Spontaneity of expression was to
become henceforth more appreciated than the photographic
exactitude of a drawing.

Still, it is difficult to delimit impressionism, since each of its
protagonists demonstrated such an independent spirit. The desire for modernity, which seemed their goal at first, was soon
abandoned by Monet, Renoir, Sisley, and Pissarro. But it guided
Manet, Degas, Berthe Morisot, and Mary Cassatt, leading them
to an expression of subjects not only essentially contemporary
but also fleeting and passing. It is there, perhaps, that the unity
of the Impressionists is greatest. For when their wish to paint
outdoors led Monet, Sisley, Renoir, and Pissarro to interpret the
phenomena of light, their themes were equally fugitive effects.
Thus, beyond the expression of the modern idea, beyond the
translation of outdoor light, beyond the seeking for a freer technique utilizing almost pure tones — which stimulated all these
artists who worked in such varied ways — is the passionate search
for the ephemeral moment lived intensely. This search unites
them all and constitutes the truest basis of impressionism.

COMMENTARY ON THE COLOR SLIDES

· 1 ·

MANET
Luncheon on the Grass
Canvas. 84¼″ x 106¼″
Signed and dated, 1863
Paris, Louvre Museum,
galleries of the
Jeu de Paume
(Moreau Nélaton Bequest)

It is often difficult for the art lover of today to understand why this painting should have caused a strange scandal at the *Salon des Refusés* in 1863. Certainly the spectacle of men dressed in contemporary clothes and juxtaposed with nude women explains an essential part of it. And yet this does not bother us today; the male costumes seem quite remote and appear no more out of place than those of the young musicians in Giorgione's *Concert Champêtre*, the celebrated work at the Louvre which certainly inspired Manet.

Nevertheless, these costumes played an important role for Manet, because they reflected his wish to be an interpreter of his time. Even though he borrowed the spirit of the scene from Giorgione and took his ideas for grouping the figures from an engraving of Marc Antonio Raimondi, the artist still wished to remain "modern." These borrowings from the past are for him only a way of working, rather than a reference to the classical spirit.

The costume was not the only new element in the painting that surprised Manet's contemporaries. The nude figure of Victorine Meurend — the model for Manet's canvas — was a greater shock. When official painters made the nude their favorite subject, they presented her under the pretext of a mythological or allegorical character, and painted her with those pleasant colors which recalled the light and sugary tones of eighteenth-century porcelain. In Manet's work, the pale flesh tones of the young woman's body seem to reflect the cold light of the artist's studio. She stands out vigorously from the canvas, firmly modeled, in striking contrast to the limp suppleness of the nudes of official paintings.

Above all, as Zola pointed out in 1867, "Manet achieved the dream that captured all the painters; to place figures of natural grandeur in a landscape." In actual fact, however, we see how in *Luncheon on the Grass* this conception is imperfect and how much the light in the canvas is still the light of an artist's studio. It was the attempt, at least, to translate the outdoor light on to canvas that struck the young painters in 1863. Nevertheless, as Zola further points out, "the crowd viewed *Luncheon on the Grass* in every way except as a masterpiece should be viewed; the crowd saw only the persons who were eating lunch on the grass after bathing, and they believed that the artist had an indecent and rowdy intention in his arrangement of the subject. Actually, the artist was simply searching to obtain lively contrasts of color and frankly stated masses."

Zola touched here on the essentials. More important than the ideas that attracted the younger painters, what really counted for Manet were the pictorial qualities of the work, its balance of masses, and the power of its rich harmonies. It is by these very qualities that the work still impresses us with great force.

2

MONET
Women in the Garden
Canvas. 100½″ x 80¾″
Painted about 1866-1867
Paris, Louvre Museum,
galleries of the
Jeu de Paume

During the summer of 1866 Monet executed this work in the village of Avray, near Paris. His wife, Camille, served as model, and it was in their own garden that he worked on this canvas. A story is told of how Monet, in order to paint more easily, dug a trench in which he could place his canvas, allowing him to reach the higher parts without using a stool.

These circumstances reveal Monet's intense desire to work in the outdoors. At this point he was already committed to doing landscapes. In the preceding year, 1865, he had finished his studies for his own great *Luncheon on the Grass*. But now it is no longer only the studies that are executed out of doors; the actual painting itself is done there.

This overriding interest led him naturally to a reworking of his palette, which had been indicated since the year before. The sharp light that bathes his figures here provokes violent contrasts by its opposition to the shadows, but it also gives these shadows a rich intensity that enchanted Monet. Thus, the harmony of his canvas was based on the contrasts of intense blues and pure whites joined with the greens of the trees.

But this concern for outdoor color effects led Monet to sacrifice interest in his model. The bright light simplifies contours, obscuring the volume of the forms in its brilliance. Camille has become no more than an elegant silhouette, not easily recognizable and, to be sure, incomprehensible to those lovers of art accustomed to the technique of official art.

If Manet's *Luncheon on the Grass* posed the problem of impressionism, Monet's *Women in the Garden* constitutes the first attempt to resolve it.

3

MORISOT
Sur la Falaise aux Petites Dalles
(The Green Parasol)
Canvas. 15¾″ x 18¼″
Painted in 1867
Cleveland Museum of Art
(Gift of the Hanna Fund)

After studying with Corot, Berthe Morisot was a student of Manet and then later became his sister-in-law. As a result of this, and also because of the influence of Monet and Renoir, she joined sympathetically in the quest for a new type of painting, becoming equally attracted to the idea of painting out of doors.

This charming canvas lies halfway between the art of Monet and that of Manet. Berthe Morisot interprets here the effect of full light on the face of her sister, Madame Pontillon, in a Norman landscape near Petites Dalles. The white robe vibrates against the green background of the meadow and creates blue shadows. But the tonality of the grass itself seems chosen more to harmonize with other elements of the picture rather than translated directly from the artist's vision of nature; it is here that we see the lesson Morisot learned from the subtle colorist Manet.

Nevertheless, the background, consisting of a sunny field of wheat cut through with clumps of grass, is closer to impressionism. The freshness of a direct notation expresses itself more fully in this background.

The whole work bears the imprint of a delicacy and charm which make it a feminine painting, through the elegance of the silhouette, its serene composition, and especially its refined harmonies.

· 4 ·

MANET
Luncheon in the Studio

Canvas. 47¼″ x 60⅝″
Painted in 1868
Munich, Bavarian State
Picture Collections

In 1868 Manet spent the summer near the sea at Boulogne. In the dining room of the house which he occupied there, the painter posed his brother-in-law Léon Koella, before a half cleared table. It is a simple subject, yet "modern" in the sense that it depicts a simple bourgeois interior.

With this subject, the painter seems to renew a kinship with the tradition of intimate painting of the Dutch masters and their fine evocations of interior light. But we may think also of Chardin here and of his figures caught in a moment of meditation that arrests them in mid-action.

The entire composition is organized about the silhouette of the young man. Around him various forms of still life are arranged in a mysterious and poetic interplay. The painter refines his tones and even the textures of his painting in order to evoke the materiality of the objects and to make them vibrate in the light.

Anecdote is thus banished, and the charm of the work lies in the relationships of tones and forms. Only the young man imposes himself on us as a person; still, his closed face seems without a soul, for it is his costume and especially the black area which carries his presence. The maidservant and the smoker are reduced to simple silhouetted elements of the still life.

Manet reduces much of the content of the subject, so that he can give more freedom to the pictorial effects. It is certainly not a new attitude in painting, for we see it also in the works of Frans Hals, Velásquez, and Chardin. But what counted, no doubt, in the eyes of the young artists — the future impressionists — was that a familiar composition owed its coherence now to a luminous unity, to the keenness and truth of its notation.

· 5 ·

MONET
The River

Canvas. 32″ x 39¼″
Painted in 1868
Chicago, The Art Institute
(Potter Palmer Collection)

Even the theme of *The River* is characteristic of the impressionists' new interests. The site chosen in this case has nothing of the picturesque in it. Even Daubigny, the painter of rivers *par excellence*, would not have chosen a view so banal, where neither the bank nor the water is clearly distinguishable. The reason is that the site itself has lost its importance in the eyes of the painter and is no longer the real subject.

The contrast of shadow and light which separates the tree in the foreground from the river bank, the contrast of the houses and their reflections in the water — such are the real themes of this rich composition. They reunite and develop further the ideas found in *Women in the Garden*. The feminine silhouette that marks the foreground is not anecdotal; because of the light colors that she brings to this area, she serves solely as a juncture between the shaded and light areas.

It is significant that we see the painter turning toward water as a subject, seeking to interpret the reflections of color values. Nowhere else would he be better able to study the intensity of tones resulting from such full light. Moreover, Monet finds there a subject where the drawing forms become secondary, giving way to an intensity and variety of colors which vibrate in a brilliant symphonic effect.

· 6 ·

RENOIR
La Grenouillère

Canvas. 29¹³⁄₁₆″ x 37¹³⁄₁₆″
Painted in 1869
Stockholm, National
Museum

During the years 1868 and 1869, Monet and Renoir often worked at Bougival, on the shore of the Seine. A garden café, La Grenouillère, where one could see boaters and bathers, attracted the two painters because of its great life and animation. Each of the artists painted many canvases of this subject, often interpreting the view from an identical angle.

The two men here pursued their studies of water reflections and evolved their techniques in a decisive manner. In order to translate better the glittering, moving colors on the vibrant water, they placed side by side small touches of pigment which broke up the surface into its color values. The drawing of reflections having been shattered by the movement of the water, the river thus became an animated surface of a thousand colors.

But for Renoir as for Monet, these paintings are still only studies and not completed works. Monet, in a letter to Bazille, stated his desire — and Renoir's too — to create a "painting, the beaches of La Grenouillère" for which, he said, he had made "some bad sketches." Neither Renoir nor Monet, then, was yet conscious of having found his true mode of expression, but their studies out of doors led them to it.

The style of the two painters is already clearly differentiated. While Monet searches in his compositions for cold harmonies, Renoir prefers a scale of warm colors. Monet likes to create his forms in colored touches; Renoir prefers a more precise suggestion and outlines his figures with a liveliness that reveals a profound sensitivity to human anecdote.

· 7 ·

SISLEY
The Saint-Martin
Canal

Canvas. 19⅝″ x 25⅝″
Signed and dated, 1870
Paris, Louvre Museum,
galleries of the
Jeu de Paume
(Gachet Bequest)

At the Salon of 1870 — the official one in which the young artists still wished to participate — Sisley showed two views of the Saint-Martin canal. By choosing this subject, Sisley presented himself as a landscapist and also as a modern painter who wanted to describe contemporary life, even in its aspects that were then considered vulgar. None the less, he is still very much attached to the conception of landscape as viewed by the older masters, and he knows, in his motif, how to associate the picturesque with a classical composition: here, the centralized perspective so much loved by Corot.

His palette, however, is light and brilliant; the surface of the water is interpreted by the contrasting vibration of multiple juxtaposed small touches of paint. Sisley thus follows closely the researches of his friends and employs here the technique discovered by Monet and Renoir the preceding year. Nevertheless, he knows how to utilize this technique with a delicacy and sense of restraint which characterizes his art and confers on his work a completely personal distinction.

Moreover, even while this brilliant and truly impressionist technique is used to evoke the water, we notice how houses, sky, and clouds are still solidly interpreted, with their surfaces clearly delineated, only accented by lively colors.

· 8 ·

PISSARRO
The Station at Penge
Canvas. 20¹³⁄₁₆″ x 32⅛″
Signed and dated, 1871
London, Courtauld
Institute

During the war of 1870, while Pissarro was a refugee in England, he painted this canvas showing a railroad station near London. The subject of railroad stations greatly attracted the impressionist painters. In it they saw a particularly modern theme, a typical expression of the introduction of the machine — that is to say, much of the ugliness — in contemporary life. But this machine also captivated the artists because of the picturesque quality of the wreaths of smoke pouring from its engines.

This work still owes much to tradition. Even if railroad tracks here have replaced the precious roads of Corot or the rivers of Daubigny, the painting is yet rigorously composed around an axial perspective: the mass of the bank on the right is quite nicely balanced by the two trees on the left and the plumes of smoke which pierce the sky.

The work is, however, a subtle notation of atmosphere which betrays the fact that it has been worked on outdoors. With the use of small brush strokes, Pissarro analyzes the nuances of color in the light sifted through a grey sky hiding the sun. He knows how to associate in happy balance a precise analysis of light, and a clear projection of forms in space.

· 9 ·

MONET
Impression, Mist
Canvas. 21⅜″ x 29½″
Signed and dated, 1872
Paris, Marmottan Museum

"What does this canvas represent? Look in the catalogue. *Impression, Rising Sun.* Impression, of that I am sure. I also say to myself, since I am very impressed, there must be somewhere down deep an impression . . . and what freedom, what ease in the technique! paper painted only in the most embryonic way is still more finished than this marine painting."

This is what Louis Leroy, the art critic of *Charivari*, had to say in 1874 when he commented — in an imaginary dialogue between an academic painter and himself — on one of the canvases of the first exhibition held by the young impressionist painters. It has long been believed that the work indicated is the one which is reproduced here.

Monet tries then for the first time to interpret in painting the effects of mist on a surface of water. The forms become blurred, space becomes confused, and the sun bursts out at certain points in vibrant colored spangles, which scintillate on a grey curtain. The "subject" or theme, as it was defined in the studies of the nineteenth century, has disappeared. The canvas is no longer "finished," as Louis Leroy would have liked it, for the elements of the view are no longer delineated by clear concise drawing. What remains is only a study of light and of colors, executed by short brush strokes which have nothing in common with the smooth technique of the official painters.

The title of the work, *Impression, Mist*, signifies the intentions of the painter. The theme is fog, and the canvas interprets a visual impression of it. Monet thus paints what he sees before him and not what he actually knows about the site enveloped by fog, the port of Le Havre. He wishes to be an "eye" and tries to interpret directly the "vision" of this eye without submitting it to the interpretation of his mind.

· 10 ·

MONET
Regatta at Argenteuil

Canvas. 18¹³⁄₁₆″ x 28¾″
Painted around 1872
Paris, Louvre Museum,
galleries of the
Jeu de Paume
(Caillebotte Bequest)

Argenteuil is a name closely associated with impressionism, and it is there that Monet painted this work around 1872. Argenteuil is the Seine, first of all, but it is also the white sails of regattas which stand out against the sky and water. From this combination, the impressionist painters created a number of luminous variations.

Monet composes this canvas without any concern for traditional perspective. It has a simple horizontal rhythm formed by movements of the water and streaks of cloud in the sky, in contrast to the vertical darting of the white sails. It is a harmony of blues, of intense blues, interrupted only by the white splashes of the sails and the red touches of two houses and their reflections.

Light permeates all of the work, shadows are absent. Almost pure colors are applied to the canvas in large patches which create forms by reason of their singular thickness. The very character of these brush strokes underlines how far Monet's technique is removed from all systems, so much so that this work is in contrast to the artist's *Impression, Mist.*

· 11 ·

CÉZANNE
The House of Père Lacroix

Canvas. 28½″ x 24″
Painted around 1873
Washington, National
Gallery of Art
(Chester Dale Collection)

It is only during his eighteen months at Auvers-sur-Oise that Cézanne created works that can really be qualified as impressionist. *The House of Père Lacroix* is one of the most important of these. It was, perhaps, one of the two "landscapes of Auvers" that the artist presented in the exhibition of 1874 in the old studio of the photographer Nadar.

The subject is certainly typical of impressionism in its contrast between the shadow of foliage in the foreground and the façade of the house bathed in sunlight. Small strokes of the brush, often applied parallel to one another, are visible in the foreground where they serve to analyze the nuances of color and to contrast with the more compact technique used in rendering the façade of the house.

The personality of Cézanne is evident still, however, in this work which remains quite removed from the contemporary canvases of a Monet or a Renoir by virtue of the relatively solid forms. The chosen view is also a very personal matter with the artist, within the self-imposed limits of his field of vision. Beyond the very first luminous impression of the painting, one can see that the real subject lies in the juxtaposition of two planes — that of the green woods and plants and that of the façade with their contrasts and their interplay. The basic and lifelong motivation of the artist already appears in his works: the expression of volumes and of space by use of color. It is primarily through color that Cézanne wishes to express the relationships of the two elements of his composition and to make clear their relationship in space.

· 12 ·

DEGAS
*At the Races;
before the Stands*
Canvas| 18⅛″ x 24″
Painted around 1872 (?)
Paris, Louvre Museum,
galleries of the
Jeu de Paume

In 1866 for the first time Degas painted pictures on racecourse subjects. He became very fond of these themes, which henceforth appeared often in his work. In them he enjoyed the charm of fashionable gatherings in the open air, but he was even more sensitive to the grace and elegance of the horses' movements.

The entire composition in the present painting revolves around a few stallions. The jockey, in orange-tinted costume, and his mount form the center of this arrangement. But instead of a frontal presentation in the academic manner, instead of such aridity and banality, Degas prefers the unexpected charm of less stylized postures. Moreover, the theme here is focused around the rear view of a horse, the delicacy of whose hooves is accentuated by an awning which throws an even more delicate shadow on the ground.

A subtle but ever-present drawing underlines the contours, conferring on the totality the curious quality of a play of colored silhouettes. To the large elegant forms of the horses there are opposed the sharp accents of the umbrellas and the costumes that set the stands into motion.

The composition conveys a sense of immensity; it opens toward us, and it is toward us that the race track appears to extend, enveloping us in its meadow. In order to stress this effect, Degas does not hesitate to cut off, at the edge of the composition, the head of the horse at the right.

It is, however, not only this concern with unexpected attitudes, this search for a fugitive beauty that marks the present work as impressionist in character. The light here also plays a decisive role. It gives the composition its coloristic power and arranges the forms through the play of shadows that it evokes. Even if this color is not interpreted by an attempt to analyze its separate rays, it nevertheless still dominates the composition.

· 13 ·

DEGAS
The Pedicure
Canvas. 24″ x 18⅛″
Signed and dated, 1873
Paris, Louvre Museum,
galleries of the
Jeu de Paume
(Camondo Bequest)

Nothing in the technique of this work, seemingly, would classify it as impressionist. The strong drawing, minutely modeled, would suggest instead the influence of Ingres. But Degas's impressionism is found elsewhere.

Like Monet, Degas wanted to paint contemporary life, and this charming intimate scene testifies to that desire. He uses the composition to evoke anecdote, and through its design we are caught up into his world. The objects are cut across by the frame in the foreground in order to induce a sense of the space and to lead us into the painting.

The commonplace character of the scene, the care taken to note the picturesque details are equally significant. Degas likes to paint the charm of a fleeting moment, the beauty born of an ephemeral association of objects, persons, habits, and finally of light.

The entire composition is bathed in a carefully noted and studied light. In that respect, Degas finds himself close to the work of his friends, even if he rejects the spontaneity of their technique and vision.

· 14 ·

MANET
Argenteuil, the Boaters

Canvas. 58¾" x 51⅝"
Painted in 1874
Tournai, Musée des
Beaux-Arts

In 1874 Manet let himself come under the spell of impressionism and came to paint with his young friends at Argenteuil. He changed his style, lightening his palette still more and creating some completely new works, more frankly impressionist than any he had done previously.

The Boaters constitutes one of the most important canvases of this period. Certainly Manet remains faithful to the "modern" scene, the evocation of contemporary society; in this case, it is some Parisians at an outing on the Seine. Nevertheless, the presentation of his couple in their frontal position still recalls the composition of a work of the official salon.

But what is new for the artist is the glistening light in which he bathes the canvas, the importance of the light landscape which occupies the entire background. It is also a more spontaneous technique, allied to Monet's work at this time. For although the figures are still painted in his older controlled manner, the brush strokes in the background are lighter, Manet applying juxtaposed and contrasting pure tones to the canvas in the manner of his younger colleagues.

· 15 ·

RENOIR
*A Path Rising
in High Grass*

Canvas. 23³⁄₁₆" x 29⅛"
Painted around 1876
Paris, Louvre Museum,
galleries of the
Jeu de Paume
(Gift of Charles Comiot)

This charming work was painted in 1875 during the Argenteuil period. The theme of this composition appears, moreover, at the same time in the work of Monet, who several times and in a similar manner painted fields of poppies or figures of people seemingly almost lost in the tall grass.

What is striking here is the astonishing warmth of the dominant colors. Whereas in Monet at this time there are almost always great areas of shadows in cold tones, here in Renoir the shadow is completely eliminated. The small red touch of the umbrella, so delicately pricked out in the middle of the wheat field, is like a symbol of the radiance that fills the canvas. This is why the painting is so profoundly significant in the art of Renoir: before even his voyage to Algeria, before his moving to the Côte d'Azur, it shows the artist's profound inclination to paint not only out of doors, but, more than that, to paint in the fullest sunlight.

The very technique of this work is now dedicated to sun painting. It does not employ the short strokes of Monet. It is more subtle and varied, blending the scumbles of small bits of paint, becoming almost matter in itself.

From his earliest works, Renoir revealed himself as a painter of women. The nude became his predilection. In his first composition, he seemed to follow in the footsteps of Courbet, showing a similar taste for robust and slightly heavy forms; but he knew even then how to depict women with a delicacy and devotion that turned them into poetry.

The *Nude in the Sun* was painted around 1876, that is to say, in the full flowering of the impressionist movement. During the second exhibition of the group, in 1876, it created a scandal, which is easy to understand. Renoir takes up a classical theme here, a nude female torso, the subject which, above all others, recalls the tradition of antique sculpture. But he rejects this tradition and conceives the subject in a completely new spirit. Consequently, it is not a question here of plastic values. Renoir, before anything else, is a colorist, and he composes in terms of the vibration of the flesh colors of the model within an interlacing of shadows and lights found under trees in full summer. The strong light penetrates everywhere, lighting up the rose skin in a thousand places, making the green of the leaves sing, and finally giving the canvas a feeling of heavy summer heat.

These Renoirs are the equivalent of the landscape studies of Monet at this same time. Their aim is identical: the translation of a luminous effect in all the charm of its fugitive quality. But Renoir puts this vision at the service of a completely personal poetry, singing praises to feminine beauty in a melody stamped with his serene and unique sensuality.

At the third impressionist exhibition in 1877, Renoir presented this work now ranked among his most important paintings. However much he is attracted by landscape, Renoir constantly and instinctively returns to the human figure. For him it seems indispensable for the expression of his *joie de vivre*, the happiness which makes up the basic thread of his art.

The Moulin de la Galette was an open-air café, a tea-garden on one of the slopes of the Montmartre hill. In it, one could dance and drink. Renoir, still enchanted by the idea of painting in the open air, had come there to plant his easel and asked a few friends to pose for him. It is from this subject that he has derived a composition which might serve as an illustration of the *Vie de Bohême* of Murger.

But while his work evokes the easy pleasures of a long-gone epoch, it is also an essentially impressionist picture characteristic of the Argenteuil period of the movement. The lively summer light pierces the foliage of the trees, playing a counterpoint with the blue-tinted shadows. It creates a colored checker pattern around the people in the picture.

The luminous dazzle is so felicitously conveyed that it becomes part of the joyous atmosphere, whirling into our eyes and seeming to set in motion the waltzers momentarily arrested by the painter's brush.

In spite of the dominance of the bluish tonalities in the total color harmony, the painting does not give us the feeling of a cold light. Actually, the blues set into relief the warm tones of the light effects, so that in the end it is an impression of sun and brightness that predominates.

· 18 ·

PISSARRO
The Red Roofs

Canvas. 20¹³⁄₁₆″ x 25³⁄₁₆″
Signed and dated, 1877
Paris, Louvre Museum,
galleries of the
Jeu de Paume
(Caillebotte Bequest)

For almost two years, in 1873 and 1874, Cézanne sojourned at Auvers-sur-Oise, not far from Pissarro who was at the time living in Pointoise. The two painters worked together often, and it is this contact which influenced Cézanne to reorganize his palette and to join the supporters of "light" painting.

But a work such as *The Red Roofs,* painted in 1877, underlines nicely the fact that the painters mutually influenced one another. To be sure, the work is more impressionist than all those of Cézanne, in that it attempts to translate the privileged and fleeting moment of a brilliant burst of sun on a day at the end of winter. Each gleam of color is noted in the slightest variation of light and shadow.

Along with this luminous notation, however, there appears a solid construction of space, a restrained space closed in by the hill and the bare saplings of the foreground. This is a typically Cézannesque theme that Pissarro has developed by analysing minutely the closed, tight network of the frail trunks and their shadows, by weaving them into a transparent screen in front of some rustic, tiled houses, by playing a unique game of superimposing these two planes through variations of light and shadow.

· 19 ·

MONET
The Saint-Lazare
Railroad Station

Canvas. 29½″ x 39¼″
Signed and dated, 1877
Paris, Louvre Museum,
galleries of the
Jeu de Paume
(Caillebotte Bequest)

Like Pissarro, Monet was attracted to the subject of railroads. But when he carried out the various treatments of the *Saint-Lazare Railroad Station,* he insisted clearly on the modern theme pre-eminently, since he eliminated in these paintings all subject matter except the locomotives and station shed. It is easy to see what captured his attention here: the lively contrasts of shadow and light between the vault and its opening to the outdoors; above all, the iridescence of the clouds of vapor crossing successively the areas of shadow and rays of light.

From roses to blues to yellows, a lively palette allows the colors to play in glittering slivers on the canvas. The forms float in the dazzling light, as in the semi-obscurity. Monet utilizes fine brush strokes and his touch becomes as delicate as if he were modeling small crystals of light.

This subject engaged Monet's interest so much that he did at least a dozen treatments of the theme. Many, in fact, figured in the third exhibition of the impressionists. It is worth noting that his was the first time that the artist had been concerned with painting a subject under different light situations. But he was not yet trying to create a really coherent series, as he was to do so often later, and in the various canvases of these railroad stations, he varied the compositional form as much as the light effects.

· 20 ·

DEGAS
Dancer Bowing with Flowers

Pastel on paper.
28⅝₁₆″ x 30½″
Painted in 1878
Paris, Louvre Museum,
galleries of the
Jeu de Paume

The opera truly fascinated Degas. He was at first attracted to it through his friend, the bassoonist Dihau. In fact, around 1868, Degas painted a portrait of the musician, showing him in the middle of the orchestra pit. But in that celebrated painting at the Louvre, one can already see the legs of dancers in the upper part.

Soon, it would be not only musicians who would attract Degas but also the dancers themselves whom henceforth he would paint and sculpt as one of his chief subjects. What he particularly appreciated in them was the brilliant and unreal world in which they moved on the stage, the grace of their gestures, and the momentary poses they assumed. At the same time, he loved to discover, even to underline, the vulgarity or ugliness often revealed when they were far from their stately theatrical world or when their turn was done.

The *Dancer Bowing with Flowers* signifies this double tendency. While a gesture full of grace animates the silhouette of the dancer, her rather ugly face is cruelly deformed by the harsh glare of the footlights. All the fatigue of her ended effort can be read tragically in her pathetic face, contrasting with the splendor of her costume and the gleaming colors of the décor that can be seen in the background. Thus, the inherent pessimism in Degas is expressed in this painting. Each of his works underlines the observation that beauty can only be fleeting.

· 21 ·

CASSATT
The Loge

Canvas. 37½″ x 29¼″
Painted about 1882
Washington, National
Gallery of Art
(Chester Dale Collection)

Mary Cassatt was introduced to impressionism by Degas. From him she learned her brilliant technique and strong design. Although she later became a painter of children, in her early works she was more than happy to go along with the subjects of the fashionable world which were closer to the interests of Degas.

The theme of the loge attracted her then, and she created many variations of it. In this composition, one cannot avoid recalling the celebrated work of Renoir of 1874 (Courtauld Collection). But this later painting shows much, also, that separates the two artists. If Cassatt's subjects have not inherited Degas's bitterness, they do not, on the other hand, express that pure joy of living which typifies the work of Renoir. They are, instead, permeated by a kind of melancholy, a slight uneasiness which is entirely personal.

But the technique of these works distinguishes them even more. Here, clear drawing delineates the forms, which are expressed with a firmness reminiscent of Manet. The playing of light enhances the expression of masses and helps to give the painting its sense of power and characteristic calm.

RENOIR
Seated Bather

Canvas. 46¹³⁄₁₆″ x 36⅞″
Painted in 1885
Cambridge, Fogg Art
Museum
(Maurice Wertheim
Collection)

Around 1883 Renoir began to have doubts concerning the value of impressionism. Faced with the difficulty of reconciling an expression of volumes and a methodical analysis of light, he turned in another direction and reintroduced in his works a clear and precise drawing. It is this period in his work that has been called "Ingresque."

The *Seated Bather*, along with the *Bathers* of the Tyson Collection in Philadelphia, is one of the most important paintings of this period. A clear drawing outlines the woman's body, the very position of this body helping to emphasize its arabesque design. The modelling is brushed in lightly in order to give more importance to the line.

But, aside from the firm drawing, the color is projected in lively tonalities. The background is treated in brightly colored scumbles that recall purely impressionist notations, particularly as we observe them in the background foliage of *Nude in the Sun*. But all comparison stops after this. The body of the woman here is lighted by an equal light which allows fullness to the forms, and its sheer intensity brings out the qualities of flesh tint. Impressionism had definitely affected Renoir, opening the way for him to a range of warm colors, capable of expressing in themselves the profound love of life which stimulated the artist; we see this phenomenon here in one of its first appearances.

DEGAS
*Woman Combing her
Hair*

Pastel on paper.
31½″ x 22⅜″
Painted around 1887-1890
Paris, Louvre Museum,
galleries of the
Jeu de Paume

It was at the eighth and last exhibition of the impressionist group, in 1886, that Degas exhibited for the first time a series of canvases concerned with the nude. In his last years this theme became his major interest. It had, however, made an earlier appearance in his work. In fact, when he was still interested in historical subjects, he created in 1865, under the pretext of a theme of the Hundred Years War, an astonishing composition consisting of a grouping of nudes, *(see Figure 2)*.

Thus, his last works, like his first, take the same direction: to treat the nude, not in the stilled and stereotyped poses of academic practice but in familiar attitudes. The scene of war allowed him to use unrestrained poses; the themes of feminine toilette offered similar possibilities.

Another aspect of women that had attracted Degas since his canvas of 1865 was the colored splendor of unraveled hair. In the present painting, it becomes his principal theme, and the entire composition centers on it.

As in all his later mature works, Degas here abandons the clear and precise drawing of his earlier works. With his failing eyesight — he had become almost blind — his treatment becomes freer, and his coloring more brilliant. Upon a base whose tonality was more often somber, there burst strident lights, such as the yellows and blues of this pastel. This freedom in the interpretation of colored impressions is doubtless due in part to the research of his friends; but it goes beyond them in introducing a real interpretation rather than a description of what the artist sees, in submitting colors to the rhythm of composition, in conferring on them a directly expressive role in the postimpressionist sense.

· 24 ·

MONET
*Cathedral in the
Morning*
Canvas. 42″ x 28¾″
Signed and dated, 1894
Paris, Louvre Museum,
galleries of the
Jeu de Paume
(Camondo Bequest)

During the period at Argenteuil, the impressionists devoted themselves essentially to the pictorial expression of light. Monet remained faithful to this preoccupation, and he alone among his friends pursued this interest to its most extreme ends. When in 1877 he painted the theme of the Saint-Lazare Railroad Station several times, there appeared already — timidly, to be sure — the idea that the same motif would be entirely transformed by different lighting during the day.

It is this idea which took hold of Monet around 1890 and gave birth to the realization of a series depicting successively haystacks, poplars along the Epte, and finally the portals of the cathedral at Rouen. This last series was particularly dear to him, and he spent two years on it, from 1892 to 1894.

He rented a room whose window opened directly on the façade of the cathedral, and it is there that he began twenty canvases which illustrated the variations of light at different hours of the day.

The choice of his theme was perhaps willingly paradoxical. Late Gothic architecture presents to the eye a complex design, a play of volumes which Monet wished to show being dissolved progressively in the light. But the depth of the portals and bays of the façade brought to him also the richness of the great gaps of their shadows, sources of contrast and juxtaposition colored with the full light of the façade.

The technique reveals the long hours of work involved here: it is a strange masonry of paint wherein the tones are imposed, one upon another, creating their fine nuances. For these works — which were to have been the translation of an essentially fleeting impression — actually were the object of a long elaboration and were only finally finished in the studio of the artist. Thus, even though Monet wanted to remain faithful to objective pictorial vision, here he already made an interpretation of that vision. More or less unconsciously, he followed a path that would again allow imagination to play a large part in art.